D0803184

NATIVE NATIONS OF THE
PLAINS

BY ANITA YASUDA

The Child's World®

Published by The Child's World®
1980 Lookout Drive • Mankato, MN 56003-1705
800-599-READ • www.childsworld.com

Acknowledgments
The Child's World®: Mary Berendes, Publishing Director
Red Line Editorial: Editorial direction and production
The Design Lab: Design
Content Consultant: Richard Meyers, PhD, Tribal Relations
Director, Program Coordinator of American Indian Studies,
South Dakota State University

Photographs ©: Jerry Burnes/Williston Herald, cover, 2
(left); U.S. Department of Defense, 1, 2 (right), 9; J. Scott
Applewhite/AP Images, 3 (top), 20; Brennan Linsley/AP
Images, 3 (middle top), 24–25; Stephen Slocomb/iStockphoto,
3 (middle bottom), 26; Josh Reynolds/AP Images, 3 (bottom),
32; Shutterstock Images, 5; Marilyn Angel Wynn/Nativestock
Pictures/Corbis, 6; North Wind Picture Archives, 8; Frances
Benjamin Johnston/Library of Congress, 11; BG Smith/
Shutterstock Images, 12, 39; Aaron L. Barth, 13; Catherine
Karnow/Corbis, 14; Peter Turnley/Corbis, 16; Harris and
Ewing/Library of Congress, 18–19; Kathryn Stevens/Star-
Tribune/AP Images, 22; Photos.com/Thinkstock, 28; Andrew
Cullen/Reuters/Corbis, 30; Jerry Hopman/iStockphoto,
31; David Ball/Corbis, 34; Paul Morigi/The Smithsonian's
National Museum of the American Indian/AP Images, 36–37

ISBN: 9781634070348
LCCN: 2014959805
Printed in the United States of America
Mankato, MN
July, 2015
PA02269

ABOUT THE AUTHOR

Anita Yasuda is the author of more than 100 books for children. She enjoys writing biographies, chapter books, and books about science and social studies. Anita lives with her family and dog in Huntington Beach, California.

A dancer performs at the Standing Rock Sioux Reservation.

TABLE OF CONTENTS

ARCTIC OCEAN

GREENLAND

Gulf of Alaska

PACIFIC OCEAN

Hudson Bay

CANADA

ATLANTIC OCEAN

UNITED STATES

KEY

Plains Native Nations

N
W   E
S

MEXICO

Gulf of Mexico

CHAPTER ONE

NATIVE NATIONS OF THE PLAINS

The plains sweep across North America from the Mississippi River to the Rocky Mountains. From central Texas, they push northward into the Canadian provinces of Alberta and Saskatchewan. This vast land is covered by many types of grasses.

The American bison is an iconic animal of the plains and a key part of Plains Nations culture. It was nearly driven to extinction by the beginning of the 20th century, but today populations are recovering.

*Members of the Crow Nation and other Plains Nations share and celebrate their culture today at **powwows** and other events.*

Slow-moving rivers such as the Missouri sweep through its wide river valleys. The dry land makes farming very hard, and the Native Peoples who first settled here focused on hunting and gathering.

The plains region has been home to approximately 30 Native Nations for thousands of years. Many nations continue to live in towns and cities and on **reservations** in the region. They include the Crow, Blackfeet, Cheyenne, Comanche, Arapaho, Sioux, Mandan, and Pawnee. Each has its own rich history, language, and stories.

Researchers believe the first groups of people came to North America from Asia. Between 10,000 and 8,000 BC, an ice age ended and **glaciers** began to shrink. Large animals such as mammoths died out. Smaller animals such as bison became common. At one time, as many as 60 million bison thundered across the plains. For more than 11,000 years, ancestors of modern Plains Nations hunted these animals. They used the bison for food, shelter, and tools. They held ceremonies honoring the bison.

Many groups traveled the grasslands following the bison as they migrated. People adapted to this life by living in cone-shaped **tepees**. A few nations hunted and farmed on the northern plains. They lived in villages. They built circular homes called lodges with earth and wooden posts. Life on the plains changed at the end of the 16th century, when the Spanish brought horses to the Americas. Horses made hunting easier. Just as the

bison were, horses were honored with song and dance.

From the early 1800s, the U.S. government believed it owned the plains. The government and white settlers did not respect the Native Peoples who had lived there for centuries. The government encouraged white settlers to go west to grow crops and build

For thousands of years, tribes of the plains including the Blackfeet used the cliffs near Fort Macleod, Alberta, as a buffalo jump. Plains Indians used to drive bison over the edge to kill them. At that time, they did not have horses or guns, which later made it easier for people to hunt bison. Men dressed as animals herded the bison toward the cliffs. At a nearby camp, people hung the bison meat in the sun to dry. They pounded the meat together with berries to make **pemmican**. They turned the hide and bones into clothing, tools, and weapons.

homes, pushing out the Native Peoples. Plains Nations saw their land and the bison disappear. Faced with starvation and diseases to which they had no **immunity**, thousands died. Eventually, government policies tore Plains Nations from their lands and moved them onto reservations. The nations lost access to their sacred lands. They could not practice many religious ceremonies that were tied to the land.

Students at Lower Brule High School on the Lower Brule Sioux Reservation created this medicine wheel. The sacred symbol represents the knowledge of the universe and has health and healing properties.

Plains Nations have had to fight for their rights and for the land to be returned to them. In 1978, a new law protected Native access to traditional sacred lands. Now nations have their own systems of government. Elected tribal councils are in charge of daycare, education, and other services on reservations. They run businesses from farming and cattle to tourism and gaming. Native languages are taught in the tribes' own schools. Important traditions such as the Sun Dance continue to be passed from one generation to the next.

CROW

A Crow woman leads a ceremonial circle at a powwow featuring members of many tribes.

Similar to many Native people, the Crow now live in towns and cities across the United States. Some call the reservation on the rolling plains of southeastern Montana home. The Crow Nation is also called *Apsaalooké*. This means "children of the large-beaked bird."

The Crow have nearly 12,000 registered members. Each Native Nation has its own set of rules for membership. Usually, a person must be related to someone on the tribe's original members list. This is called a base roll. People are asked to enroll to protect a tribe's unique character. Approximately 75 percent of Crow members live on or near the 2.3 million acre (930,000 ha) reservation. It is the largest in Montana. The nation has coal, oil, and gas reserves. Some members farm or ranch.

dog	bishké	(by-sh-kay)	
horse	iichíile	(ai-chai-lay)	SAY IT
bison	bishée	(by-shay)	
wolf	chéete	(chay-tay)	

Crow young and old celebrate their culture at the annual rodeo called Crow Fair. It is their longest-running contemporary celebration. People come to see the hundreds of horses and thousands of tepees. They cheer on riders in the all-Native rodeo and watch the dance competitions. Some men wear traditional Crow **war bonnets**. These headdresses are made with golden eagle feathers.

In the past, there were few jobs on the reservation. The tribal government is trying to change this. The Crow have gone into business with Cloud Peak Energy of Wyoming to create jobs. The company hopes to mine up to 10 million tons (9 million metric tons) of coal a year.

The teaching of Crow history, culture, and language is important to their people. From the late 19th to the first half of the 20th century, the U.S. government tried to wipe

Residential school students dressed in nonnative clothing and spoke English.

out Native culture. One way was through **residential schools**. Native children were taken from their homes. Teachers forbade them from speaking their own languages or practicing their cultures. Children suffered years of abuse. Many died from diseases such as measles, which spread quickly in the boarding schools.

Now nations including the Crow are in charge of their children's education. In elementary schools children learn Crow through song. They sign words using Plains Indian sign language. Plains Nations created this language centuries ago. It helped them communicate with groups that spoke other languages.

CHAPTER THREE

BLACKFEET

Chief Mountain rises at the western edge of the Blackfeet reservation. The 1.5 million acre (600,000 ha) reservation in northwestern Montana borders Canada. It is bigger than the state of Delaware. The Blackfeet Nation has approximately

The Blackfeet have lived near Chief Mountain for thousands of years.

17,500 members, and 10,000 live on the reservation. The Blackfeet once controlled the northeastern plains from the North Saskatchewan River in Canada to the Missouri River in Montana. They organized themselves into bands that usually lived apart. Important ceremonies such as the Sun Dance brought the bands together.

The Sun Dance, held between late spring and mid-summer, remains an important ceremony. Blackfeet come to celebrate the earth and their continued good health. Over four days, people fast and pray. On the last day, several dances take place around a tall pole. The pole draws the dancers' attention up to the Creator. As they dance, people say prayers for their family, community, and the earth. The ceremony ends with a feast.

Born on the Blackfeet reservation, artist Jay Polite Laber creates sculptures from scrap metal.

Children learn the Blackfeet language and cultural heritage at a school on the Blackfeet reservation in Montana.

Once, the Blackfeet led a **nomadic** life. Horses pulled their supplies and tepees on **travois**. Now some own cattle farms. These farms are an important source of income for the Montana reservation. The community, located on the edge of Glacier National Park, relies on tourism and its casino. The reservation also leases land to oil companies. The nation has invested heavily in education and operates the Blackfeet Community College.

In Canada, the Piikani (or Northern Peigan), Kainai, and Siksika Nations make up the Blackfoot Confederacy. They call themselves *Niitsitapi*. This means "original people." The Kainai have the largest **reserve** in all of Canada. Rich deposits of oil and gas on their land have led to business partnerships with energy companies. The reserve leases land to neighboring farmers. A factory processes hay for sale. The Piikani operate a factory that makes moccasins and other goods. Members also work at Head-Smashed-In Buffalo Jump World Heritage Site.

The Siksika attract tourists with a new museum and the annual World Chicken Dance competition each summer. The dance, called *Kitokipaaskaan*, imitates the mating dance of a chicken. It is told that a chicken came to a man in a dream after the man ate it. The chicken threatened to kill the man's family if he did not teach the dance to others. This dance began in this area but is now seen at Native celebrations throughout North America.

CHAPTER FOUR

CHEYENNE

Ben Nighthorse Campbell of the Northern Cheyenne was the third Native American elected to the U.S. Senate, serving from 1993 to 2005.

Cheyenne live across the United States. Some Southern Cheyenne live with the Arapaho on a reservation in central Oklahoma. Many Northern Cheyenne live on the rugged lands of southeast Montana. This reservation includes 440,000 acres

(180,000 ha) of grasslands. More than 9,000 nation members live there. The ten-member council and a president govern the nation. The Cheyenne call themselves *Tsitsistas*. The word has a several meanings, including "our people."

The Northern Cheyenne reservation has many natural resources, including 56 billion tons (51 billion metric tons) of coal. Though the unemployment rate is at least 60 percent and mining provides many jobs, not all members support mining. They worry about how mining damages the land. A few members find employment with the Saint Labre Indian School. Construction companies, an arts center, ranching, and a small casino are sources of jobs, too.

The Sacred Arrows and the Sacred Buffalo Hat are important objects in Cheyenne culture. Both objects have a full-time Keeper. It is the Keeper's job to pray to the objects for the well-being of the Cheyenne. It is told that more than 1,000 years ago, gods gave four Sacred Arrows to Sweet Medicine, a holy man. Two arrows were for war and two were for hunting. If the tribe showed respect to the arrows through ceremonies, it would prosper. The Southern Cheyenne of Oklahoma keep the Sacred Arrows.

The Sacred Buffalo Hat came from the Suhtai tribe. In the early 19th century, the Suhtai became part of the Cheyenne. The Sacred Buffalo Hat stays with the Northern Cheyenne in Montana. Before a journey, some Cheyenne visit the Sacred Hat with gifts such as tobacco. It is a way of asking the power of the Sacred Hat to keep them safe when they are far from home.

A little more than 1,000 people speak Cheyenne in Montana. The number of speakers in Oklahoma is fewer. The Cheyenne are trying to keep their language alive. Cheyenne is taught in Oklahoma at Watonga High School. Language camps for older students began in 2014. There are also online classes.

In the 19th century, the U.S. government and settlers did not show respect for Native American culture. Important Native objects and human remains were taken and sold. In 1986, members of the Northern Cheyenne discovered the Smithsonian Institution held more than 18,000 Native remains. The remains were being kept in drawers as if they were objects rather than human beings. The Northern Cheyenne demanded that the remains be returned to their tribes for burial. Their concerns sparked a movement that resulted in important laws. The most important is the Native American Graves Protection and Repatriation Act. Now all Native remains, sacred objects, and objects connected to burial must be returned to their proper Native community. The laws also led to the creation of the National Museum of the American Indian in Washington, D.C.

Cheyenne leaders visited the U.S. president in 1924. Representatives from many nations discussed treaty violations with the government during this era.

CHAPTER FIVE

COMANCHE

Comanche family members of World War II code talkers received the Congressional Gold Medal, a high honor, in 2013.

The Comanche call themselves *Nermernuh*, meaning "people." Many Comanche people live in Oklahoma and Texas. There are more than 15,000 members. The Comanche do not have a reservation. However, they have a government based near Lawton, Oklahoma, and the nation owns some land. The Comanche Nation runs many community programs. Members also supply food to low-income Native families in the Lawton, Oklahoma, area.

The Comanche Nation College is located in Lawton. For more than ten years, the college has hosted a Native film festival. Talented Native directors and writers showcase their work there.

Once the Comanche lived in a huge area of land called the *Comancheria*. They were known as excellent horse breeders and had some of the biggest herds on the plains. From the mid-1800s, Native Peoples including the Comanches were forced off their land and onto reservations to make way for white settlers. In 1887, the Dawes Act passed. U.S. officials wanted to turn Native Peoples into farmers. Reservation land was broken up between families. Other lands were sold. Though the Comanches protested, the government opened the rest of their reservation to white settlers. They soon outnumbered the Comanches. But many Comanche families still live on the land they were granted.

During World War II (1939-1945), the U.S. Army recruited 17 Comanche men to train as code talkers. A code talker translated army messages into Comanche to frustrate the enemy. Thirteen men of the Comanche served in Europe with the U.S. Army's Fourth Infantry. The men used everyday Comanche words for military words. They communicated with each other via radio or telephone. Messages were then written in English and given to the officer in charge. The enemy was never able to break the Comanche code. The last Comanche code talker, Charles Chibitty, died in 2005. Both the French and U.S. governments recognized him for his contributions to the war effort.

CHAPTER SIX

ARAPAHO

The Arapaho Nation is split between the Southern and Northern Arapaho. *Arapaho* may come from a Pawnee word meaning "trader." They call themselves *Inuna-ina*, meaning "our people."

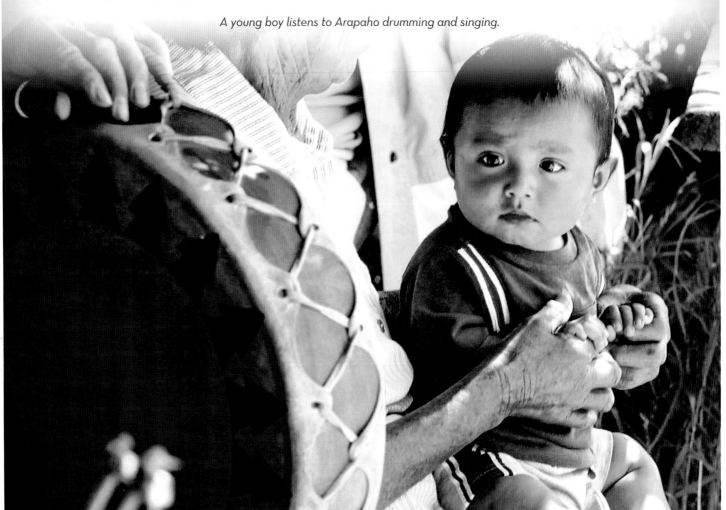

A young boy listens to Arapaho drumming and singing.

The Southern Arapaho and Southern Cheyenne have a joint government. It is located in Concho, Oklahoma. Since 2012, the groups have run a television station from the Concho headquarters. Their station, CATV47, is the first Native run and owned broadcast TV station in Oklahoma.

Together the Cheyenne and Arapaho also run many cultural programs for members. One of these important events is the Sand Creek Massacre Spiritual Healing Run. The run began in 2000. It is held in memory of the Sand Creek Massacre. In 1864, the U.S. Cavalry attacked a Cheyenne and Arapaho village. Nearly 200 people were killed. Most of the dead were women, children, and the elderly.

The Northern Arapaho live with the Eastern Shoshone on the Wind River Reservation in Wyoming. Approximately 14,000 people live there. For more than 60 years, the Northern Arapaho Celebration has been held each summer. It is Wyoming's oldest powwow, and the sounds of drums and singing fill the air for days. Dancers compete in several divisions, such as the Men's Grass Dance. This energetic dance sees men mimic the long prairie grass.

SAY IT

book	wo3ónohoe	(wo-on-hie)
table	bíí3ihíitóo	(pi-shi-aw)
chair	3í'okúutóo	(f-ku-aw)
bag	ce'éiinox	(ch-ayy-nok)
food	bíí3wo	(pi-wau)

The Wind River Reservation is known for its high unemployment and poverty. This has made the community vulnerable to substance abuse and suicide. Many other nations are struggling with similar problems. There is no simple solution. Some Native leaders believe that building stronger connections to community and culture will help members overcome addiction. The Arapaho are working hard to heal their community. Wind River Reservation's youth council encourages young people to build strong ties to their culture through music, dance, and feasts. It is hoped a strong foundation will prevent abuse and help youth be successful.

Arapaho and Cheyenne members marked the 150th anniversary of the Sand Creek Massacre in 2014.

CHAPTER SEVEN

SIOUX

The Morning Star Riders, made up of members of the Sioux and Cheyenne Nations, remember their ancestors' victory over U.S. Army leader George Armstrong Custer at the Battle of Little Bighorn in 1876.

The *Oceti Sakowin* is also known as the Sioux Nation. It is a confederacy of different groups. Members speak three different **dialects**—Dakota, Nakota, and Lakota. The Sioux Nation has reservations in many states and provinces. Sioux bands in Canada live on reserves in Alberta, Saskatchewan, and Manitoba. The Lakota have reservations in South and North Dakota. The Dakota live in South Dakota, Minnesota, and Nebraska. North and South Dakota and Montana are home to the Nakota.

Sioux Nation bands are working to gain control of their lands and chart their own economic future. In 2013, the Sioux Valley Dakota in Manitoba reached a new agreement with the Canadian government. After talks that lasted 20 years, the band became self-governing. They are the first nation on the plains to do so. Dakota, Lakota, and Nakota communities in the United States run many kinds of businesses to create jobs for members. This is very important, as reservations in North and South Dakota are some of the poorest areas in the United States. In the 1980s, Pine Ridge Reservation in South Dakota established Lakota Funds to fight poverty. It funds new and upcoming businesses. Loan money has helped many businesses from micro-farms to bakeries. Since the program began in 1986, more than 1,300 jobs have been created.

In the late 1800s, some members of the Sioux Nation began practicing a new ceremony, the Ghost Dance. The Ghost Dance was meant to bring back the bison and restore tribal lands. The U.S. government did not understand the ceremony and banned it. As part of this ban, they came to arrest Chief Big Foot of the Miniconjou Lakota. The Seventh Cavalry confined his band to Wounded Knee Creek in the Pine Ridge Reservation. On December 29, 1890, the cavalry opened fire while collecting weapons from the camp. U.S. soldiers killed more than 150 Lakota in the massacre.

Amos Bad Heart Bull's drawings from the 19th century recorded Sioux history from the time.

Some Sioux reservations such as the Flandreau Santee Sioux Tribe have casinos. Other tribes are turning to natural resources. Six Sioux tribes including the Crow Creek Sioux are developing the largest wind farm in the United States. The Lower Brule Sioux have a vast wildlife reserve with 300 bison. They are also one of the top popcorn producers in the United States.

Sioux artists show their work around the world. For more than 50 years, artist and educator Arthur Amiotte of the Oglala Lakota band has been creating powerful collages.

His pieces are found at the Smithsonian Institute and the South Dakota Art Museum. Amiotte uses his Lakota heritage, modern images such as cars, and humor to inspire his work. His artwork shows how new ideas and technology are now part of Lakota culture. Sometimes his art includes Native Americans driving cars. This is meant to show that they are in control of where they are going.

hawk	četaŋ	(cheh-tahn)
coyote	mayasleca	(mah-yah-shleh-chah)
otter	ptaŋ	(ptan)
prairie dog	pispisza	(pish-pee-zah)

SAY IT

CHAPTER EIGHT

MANDAN

The Fort Berthold Reservation in North Dakota is home to the Mandan Nation. They live there with the Hidatsa and the Arikara. Together, they are known as the Three Affiliated Tribes. The reservation has approximately 4,000 residents on 980,000 acres (400,000 ha).

Oil wells in the Fort Berthold Reservation bring in income for the Three Affiliated Tribes.

On-a-Slant Village in North Dakota features reconstructed earth lodges similar to those the Mandan lived in hundreds of years ago.

Once, the Mandan lived in villages where they built earth lodges. They farmed the land and grew many types of crops, including corn, beans, and squash. Now, new industries such as mining have replaced agriculture. The reservation has rich oil reserves. Before the Three Affiliated Tribes began producing oil, the unemployment rate on the reservation

In 2011, Edwin Benson was the only remaining Mandan speaker in Twin Buttes, North Dakota, a village that sheltered Lewis and Clark in 1804. The painted bison robe is from the 19th century.

was 70 percent. Now, there are so many jobs that people from other nations and nonnatives are employed. The reservation produces more than 330,000 barrels of oil a day. That is almost equal to the entire state of Oklahoma's daily production. In the next ten years, the Mandan hope to drill 1,000 more wells. The tax revenue on the oil brings in millions of dollars each month.

Some of the oil revenue goes to build roads and bridges. It also funds education, health, and arts programs in the community. One artist, Mildred Jordt, produces star quilts. The star represents new beginnings. Jordt's quilt of Sacagawea hangs in the Three Affiliated Tribes Museum. Sacagawea, a Shoshone woman who had been captured by the Hidatsa, was an important part of Meriwether Lewis and William Clark's team mapping the West. They met her in 1804, when the team stayed near the Mandan and Hidatsa villages for a winter. She accompanied Lewis and Clark to the Pacific Ocean and back.

While spending the winter near the Mandan and Hidatsa villages, Lewis and Clark sent boxes of Native objects to Thomas Jefferson. One item was a robe from Mandan Chief Black Cat. Jefferson displayed some of the objects at Monticello, his home. After his death, the objects disappeared. In 2002, Native American artists were asked to recreate items from the collection. One of those artists was Dennis R. Fox Jr. from the Three Affiliated Tribes. He made a painted buffalo robe based on his studies of traditional techniques. Once, leaders wore buffalo hides painted with images. The images told of their bravery and of important events such as battles in the tribe's history.

CHAPTER NINE

PAWNEE

A Pawnee Nation member participates in Oklahoma City's Red Earth Native American Cultural Festival, an annual art and cultural show.

Crops of corn and wheat cover the plains of Pawnee County in north-central Oklahoma. The area is home to the majority of the 3,000 members of the Pawnee Nation of Oklahoma. Members are split into four bands. They are the Chaui, the Kitkehahki, the Pitahawirata, and the Skidi.

The Pawnee Nation generates income and creates jobs for members through several businesses. The nation owns two casinos, a restaurant, and a gas station. The nation is working to improve services for its members. In 2013, renovations began on the tribal roundhouse. It is a place for social gatherings. Originally built in 1980, the roundhouse was modeled after a traditional earth lodge. The roof of the lodge stands for the sky, and the walls are the horizon. The tribe began construction on a new Elder Center in 2014. During the summer, the Pawnee Nation's Youth Services Department offers Pawnee language classes and a cultural camp. Children can hear the Pawnee creation story or learn a traditional dance.

Dance and song are an important part of community life. The Pawnee Indian Veterans Association holds an annual summer celebration. Songs are created for members who have served in the military. The songs are performed from memory. The event began in 1946 to welcome home returning World War II veterans. The dances began with warrior societies. Each warrior society has its own songs, dances, and symbols. Rituals ensured the groups' members' success. One of the war dances performed at the Pawnee celebration is the Straight Dance. The dancer's movements tell the story of a hunt or battle.

SAY IT		
hair	uúsu	(ooo-soo)
nose	cuúsu'	(coo-soo)
mouth	aáka'u'	(ah-ka-oo)
eyes	kíriiku'	(kir-ee-koo)

Respect for traditional culture is taught year-round at the Pawnee Nation College. The college offers programs from American Indian Studies to computer science. All students must take Pawnee language and cultural classes. Native Nations across the plains run similar language and culture programs for learners of all ages.

Kevin Gover of the Pawnee Tribe is the director of the Smithsonian's National Museum of the American Indian. As director, he helps preserve the history and culture of all Native Nations.

dialects (DYE-uh-lekts) Dialects are the way a language is spoken in a specific region or among a group of people. Many Native languages have several dialects.

glaciers (GLEY-shers) Glaciers are huge masses of ice that move very slowly. Glaciers are made of snow, ice, and rock.

immunity (ih-MYOO-ni-tee) Immunity is a body's ability to defend itself against germs and stay healthy. Native Peoples had little immunity to new European diseases such as smallpox.

nomadic (noh-MAD-ik) Someone who is nomadic moves from place to place. Some Plains Nations led a nomadic live.

pemmican (PEM-i-kuhn) Pemmican is a food made with dried meat and berries pressed into loaves. Pemmican is a traditional Plains Nations food.

powwows (POU-wouws) Powwows are a social gatherings of Native Americans that usually include dancing. Many Native Nations have powwows to celebrate their culture and traditions.

reservations (rez-er-VAY-shuhns) Reservations are areas of land set aside for Native use. Reservations are run by their own governments and provide services to their residents.

reserve (ree-SURV) A reserve is a piece of land set aside by the Canadian government for aboriginal use. The Blackfeet have a large reserve in Canada.

residential schools (rez-i-DEN-shuhl SKOOLS) Residential schools were boarding schools funded by the Canadian or American federal governments for Native children. Until the middle of the 20th century, many Native children were forced to go to residential schools.

tepees (TEE-pees) Tepees are cone-shaped tents made of animal skins. Some Plains Nations members lived in tepees.

travois (trah-VWAH) A travois is a device with two poles and a net or a platform used to drag items. Some Plains Nations used travois to haul items when they traveled.

war bonnets (WOR BAHN-its) War bonnets are bands decorated with feathers worn around the forehead. It is believed war bonnets will protect wearers from harm.

TO LEARN MORE

BOOKS

Gibson, Karen Bush. *Native American History for Kids: With 21 Activities.* Chicago: Chicago Review Press, 2010.

Kissock, Heather. *Comanche: American Indian Art and Culture.* New York: Weigl Publishing, 2011.

Sneve, Virginia Driving Hawk. *The Christmas Coat: Memories of My Sioux Childhood.* New York: Holiday House, 2011.

WEB SITES

Visit our Web site for links about Native Nations of the Plains:
childsworld.com/links

Note to Parents, Teachers, and Librarians: We routinely verify our Web links to make sure they are safe and active sites. So encourage your readers to check them out!